A SOLDIER'S DIARY

A Soldier's Diary

The Boer War
1899–1902

Edited by Graham Chambers

The Pentland Press Ltd
Edinburgh · Cambridge · Durham · USA

First published in 1999 by
The Pentland Press Ltd.
1 Hutton Close
South Church
Bishop Auckland
Durham

British Library Cataloguing in Publication Data.
A catalogue record for this book is available
from the British Library.

ISBN 1 85821 635 4

Typeset by George Wishart & Associates, Whitley Bay.
Printed and bound by Antony Rowe Ltd., Chippenham.

Contents

Illustrations   vii

Maps   viii

Acknowledgements   ix

Foreword   xiii

Preface   xvii

Background   xxi

Chapter I: 1899 (including the Battle of
              Colenso)   1

Chapter II: 1900 (The Battles of Vaal Krantz
             and Pieter's Hill: Relief of
             Ladysmith)   12

Chapter III: 1901 (a move towards guerilla
             warfare)   61

Chapter IV: 1902 (Blockhouses and Peace) . . .   69

Postscript   81

Epilogue   82

Bibliography   85

Index   87

Illustrations

Durham Light Infantry South African
War Memorial in Durham Cathedral
Churchyard xxvi

South Africa 1900 New Testament and
Chocolate Box 33

Private Chambers' Diary 33

Officers inspecting Outpost of 1st Durham
Light Infantry at Eden Kop 60

Short Service – Attestation of 5319 Thomas
Chambers 68

Thomas Chambers in his World War I uniform . 84

Maps

South Africa 1899–1902 xxv

Battle of Pieter's Hill 25

Acknowledgements

I am extremely grateful for the help that I have received from a number of people in producing this book. The suggestions from Stephen Shannon of the Durham Light Infantry Museum and Durham Art Gallery were much appreciated and I am grateful to the staff at Poole Library for obtaining the books I needed.

Crown copyright material (WO97/4511) in the Public Record Office is reproduced by permission of the Controller of Her Majesty's Stationery Office.

I would also like to acknowledge my thanks and appreciation to my dear friends Viv Elliot and Jim Graham, and my mother-in-law Margaret, whose help and encouragement was invaluable.

My grateful thanks are also due to Roger Norris, the Deputy Chapter Librarian of Durham Cathedral for taking the photograph of the Boer War Memorial in Durham Cathedral's north yard.

Lastly I would like to acknowledge my grandfather's initiative and vision in recording his experiences of the Boer War, without which this book could not have been written and his memories lost for ever.

To Rowena, a wonderful wife,
friend and helpmate.

Foreword

Graham Chambers has compiled from his grandfather's diaries a fascinating vignette of life in the Boer War as seen through the eyes of a private soldier. The timing of the publication of the book coincides with the centenary of the start of the war, which as the years have passed has become ever more controversial as to its objectives and its conduct. Thomas Chambers hints in his diaries at some of these controversies, showing remarkable insight for a humble soldier.

Thomas had become a regular soldier five years before his battalion was sent to South Africa. He had joined the Durham Light Infantry, one of the most distinguished regiments in the British Army. His account of his own and the battalion's adventures fills a gap in the annals of that campaign. He underlines the patriotism felt by the common man for Queen Victoria and the British Empire at its apogee of power and influence. He recounts the support by way of gifts from the British public and from commercial concerns reflecting the solicitude and encouragement shown to the Queen's forces. He adds various philosophical thoughts on the war as when he comments on the aftermath of the battle of Pieter's Hill, 'Colonels lying dead amongst the Privates. All one rank now'. Interestingly he reflects the great affection the soldiers had for General Sir Redvers Buller who was removed from overall command and to this day remains a controversial figure.

His thoughts on the Boers are consistently disparaging, generally describing them as filthy. However as the war progresses he begins to see a level of futility in it all and expresses the 'hope that the day is not too far distant when Boer and Briton shall clasp hand in hand and become brothers side by side in peace'. He is not uncritical as when he talks of 'chasing the Boer from one place to another, a rather silly game on our part I fancy, a foot soldier trying to catch a mounted one'.

Clearly for much of the time life as a soldier in war was hard, difficult, boring and uncomfortable. At times relieved by intervals of intense and dangerous activity during the battles, at other times by relative luxury such as Boxing Day 1900 when Chambers and Corporal Howe shared two bottles of champagne and a good meal on their day off duty.

Graham Chambers has produced a book which everyone interested in the private soldier's view of war will find enlightening. He has done so retaining the original language of the diaries whilst giving us a very readable account. He is to be congratulated.

Sir Alexander Graham GBE

Preface

As a teenager I was given a diary by my grandfather in which he had recorded some of his experiences whilst serving as a soldier in the Boer War.

Whilst many books have been written over the years about the war I had often since thought that, possibly, my grandfather's comments may be of interest to a wider audience, particularly as the centenary of that event approaches.

The diary was not intended to be a detailed history of the war but the recorded activities of *'just one humble soldier and immensely loyal subject amongst thousands'*. I have tried, however, to interface the daily recorded events within the context of a wider commentary of a war which S.P.G. Ward[1] commented was commonly regarded now as a faintly ludicrous and somewhat discreditable episode in our military history.

The pages that follow therefore, I hope, will be of interest to many reflecting the personal memories of Private and later Lance Corporal Thomas Chambers.

---

1 The History of the Durham Light Infantry, 1962.

In transcribing the diary I have not altered the grammar so that it reflects, possibly, not only the style of the late nineteenth/early twentieth century but also the education and in some cases the wry humour (...*we set off on another wild Boer hunt*...) of a man who started work at ten years of age.

Thomas Chambers was the youngest of six children, born in Stafford on 20 June 1875 to Hannah (née Hayward, originally from Buckingham) who died when he was just two years old, and John Chambers, a publican who ran the Vine Inn, Castle Street, Stafford but who had originally come from Great Houghton, Northampton. Thomas was only ten years of age when he started work cleaning boots and knives and became an apprentice to a builder when fourteen years old but left a year and a half later '*owing to my master's bankruptcy*'.

During the following three years or so he worked, first as a pork butcher with his brother-in-law, then had a short spell painting washing machines before spending eight months down a coal mine. He then worked as an ostler before he went to work at a brewery for eighteen months. It was at the brewery, he recalls, that he fell into a vat of boiling water which resulted in severe scalds and eight weeks in the Infirmary.

It was then his military experiences began when, on 20 October 1894 he enlisted in the 68th

Regiment – Durham Light Infantry – *'after much roaming and not much benefit'* and joined the Regiment at Newcastle on Tyne on 24 October 1894.

Private Thomas Chambers (Nö. 5319) was posted to the 1st Battalion of the Durham Light Infantry in January 1895 and served in the Officers' Mess from January 1896. During his service with the Regiment he records that he worked his way up from *'4th waiter or billiard marker to Lance Corporal head waiter'*.

According to his service records (Public Records Office, Kew) he elected to come under the provisions of Special Army Order dated 2 April 1898 for 'Messing Allowance' and in the same month went with the Regiment to Dublin.

One result of the outbreak of hostilities in the Union of South Africa in 1899 was the beginning of this small diary.

Graham Chambers   April 1998

Background

South Africa was originally inhabited by Bushmen and Hottentots. Bantus, including Sotho, Swazi, Xhosa and Zulu settled there before the seventeenth century. The Cape of Good Hope was rounded by Bartolomeu Diaz in 1488; the coast of Natal was sighted by Vasco da Gama in 1497. The Dutch East India Company founded Cape Town in 1652 as a port of call on the way to the Indies.

Occupied by Britain in 1795 and 1806, Cape Town and the hinterland were purchased by Britain in 1814 for £6 million. Britons also settled in Natal, on the coast near Durban in 1824. In 1836 some 10,000 Dutch (who had been in South Africa before the British), wishing to escape from British rule, set out north on the Great Trek and founded the Republics of Transvaal and the Orange Free State; they also settled in northern Natal, which became part of Cape Colony in 1844 and a separate colony in 1856.

The Dutch-speaking Transvaal had been given limited self-governing rights by Britain in 1852 and in 1854 similar rights were given to the Orange Free State region.

By 1877 however, the relationship between the Transvaal and the neighbouring nations of the African interior had become so fraught that the British High Commissioner in Cape Town was compelled to intervene by annexing the Transvaal and by sending troops into Zululand.

The military conquest over the Zulus and the consequent incorporation of their land brought a brief period of peace to the region which, unfortunately, only lasted until 1880.

With the threat from the Zulus removed, a rebellion of Transvaal Boers was led by Paul Kruger, who had been a persistent opponent of anything British. They inflicted defeats on the British at Laing's Nek, Mount Prospect and Majuba Hill. As a result of these reverses the British were persuaded against further involvement in the affairs of the Transvaal and restored self-government.

In 1883 Paul Kruger was elected President of the Transvaal and reverted the region to its previous path of isolation and self-sufficiency.

The year 1886 saw a change in the British attitude towards the Transvaal when gold was discovered on the Witwatersrand. This discovery resulted in the invasion by fortune seekers, many of whom were white English-speaking prospectors. They were known as Uitlanders (outsiders). This inevitably threatened the dominance of the Dutch-speaking Boers who were seeing their region elevated from being one of the poorest in the world to one of the richest. In retaliation the Boers severely restricted the rights of the newcomers by refusing them political recognition and imposing exhorbitant taxes.

In 1895 there was an abortive attempt, in support of the Uitlanders and the imperialist ambitions of Cecil Rhodes, to topple Kruger. This action became known as the Jameson Raid having been led by Leander Starr Jameson, but it only resulted in provoking even tougher Boer reaction.

The Transvaal formed a military alliance with the Orange Free State and, with the prospect of war looming, attempts were made to avoid what the Transvaal felt was inevitable.

The Transvaal's terms for avoiding war were set out in a despatch which was handed to the British Agent at Pretoria on 9 October.

The despatch, which was in the form of an ultimatum demanded:

1. Immediate withdrawal of British troops from Transvaal Border.
2. Removal from South Africa of all British reinforcements within reasonable time.

3. An arbitration committee to settle points of mutual difference.
4. An assurance by the British Government that British troops now en route for the Cape shall not be landed in any part of South Africa.

The British Government's response to the British High Commission on 10 October 1899 was as follows:

> Her Majesty's Government have received with great regret the peremptory demands of the Government of South Africa, conveyed in your telegram of 9th October, No. 3. You will inform the Government of the South African Republic in reply that the conditions demanded by Government of South African Republic are such as Her Majesty's Government deem it impossible to discuss.

The Boers declared war on 11 October 1899.

South Africa 1899–1902

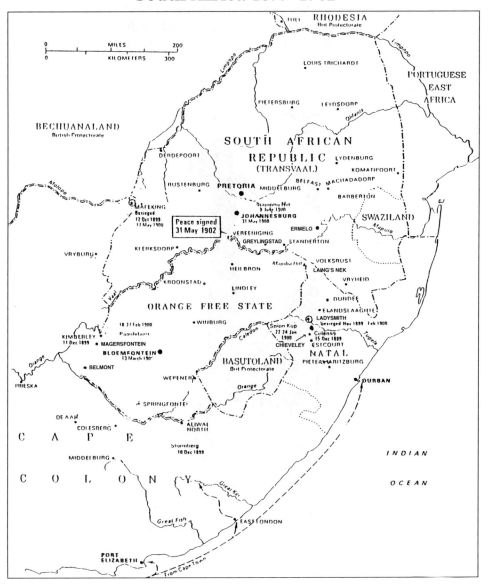

*To the memory of the officers, non-commissioned
officers and men of the Durham Light Infantry, who
were killed in action, or died of wounds or disease in
the South African Campaign 1899–1902*

'Faithful unto Death'

*Durham Light Infantry South African War Memorial in
Durham Cathedral Churchyard. Erected 1905.*

Chapter I

1899

The war started with a Boer invasion of British territory – Kimberley (under the command of Lt. Col. Robert Kekewich), and Mafeking, whose garrison was under the command of Col. Robert Stephenson Smyth Baden-Powell, being put under siege in mid-October. The British, however, had early successes at Dundee and Elandslaagte but efforts to prevent the siege of Ladysmith, which came under the command of Lt. Gen. Sir George White, in early November were unsuccessful, one small British force surrendering to the Boers at Nicholson's Nek.

The British had expected an easy victory but as events unfolded the war was to last 2½ years. The Transvaal Government had imported substantial stocks of artillery and rifles from Europe but replenishment of their arms was impossible as the Royal Navy controlled the seas and, therefore, access to the ports, and the Portuguese Government agreed to ban the passage of arms through Mozambique.

In order to break the blockades General Buller[1] left England on 14 October to take command of the British troops operating against the Boers. Some 47,000 men, including Private Thomas Chambers, also left England for duty over the next few weeks, the largest army that had ever been sent overseas from England. This included the 68th or 1st Battalion of the Durham Light Infantry (which had seen no active service in the preceding thirty-five years) who received orders early in September to prepare for service in South Africa.

Upon returning to England in 1887, after some fifteen years in India, the Battalion was based in a number of locations, including Colchester, Bradford, Lichfield and Aldershot. It embarked for Ireland in September 1893, where Headquarters and the main part of the Battalion remained for two years, with the whole Battalion moving to Dublin in 1895.

In 1898 the Battalion moved back to Aldershot where it formed part of the 2nd Infantry Brigade. However, on going abroad it was to join the 4th (Light) Brigade under Major General the Hon. N.G. Lyttleton C.B. of the 2nd Division (Lieutenant General Sir C.F. Clery, K.C.B.).

---

1 General The Right Honourable Sir Redvers Buller (1839–1908), Commander in South Africa until replaced by Lord Roberts.

24 October
We entrained at Farnborough for Southampton and arrived there quite safe and embarked on board the Cunard liner S.S. Cephalonia *for South Africa. At 6pm we left the docks amidst great enthusiasm and cheering from the spectators on the quay. We stayed off the Isle of Wight until next morning on account of the fog.*

Also on board the *Cephalonia* were Captain de Lisle (later to become General Sir H. de Beauvoir de Lisle) and two companies of the 2nd Battalion of Mounted Infantry.

25 October
At 10am we started on our long voyage in splendid weather. We were inspected by the Captain of the ship. The band played to us during the evening.

26 October
Another lovely day. We all had our kits inspected by the Company Officer.

27 October–1 November
Started to do monkey motions every morning. The Adjutant asked me if I would like a billet and I said 'yes' so all through the voyage I was Assistant Ship's Steward and fed very well. Parade every morning for the Battalion. I was struck off all duty.

2 November
*We arrived at Port St Vincent and took in coal. The
sailors helped us to coal ship and we were all like a lot of
niggers by the time it was finished, kits and everything
being covered by coal dust. The sailors, who belonged to
HMS* Diadem *seemed quite used to it. The* Pavonia,
*sister ship to ours, had just left St Vincent with the 7th
Fusiliers and the Scots Fusiliers on board.*

3 November
At 6am we left St Vincent for the Cape. We passed the
Pavonia *in the afternoon. We fired 5 rounds at some boxes
which had been thrown for targets.*

4–17 November
*Still going along with most pleasant weather. Pass a few
ships now and again – nothing of any interest except a
few porpoises, dolphins, sharks, and flying fish to be seen,
until we land at the Cape and disembarked 300 Mounted
Infantry and some R.A.M.C. Here we coaled ship again,
being done by niggers, when we stopped for two days.*

*Spent most of that stay watching the seagulls dropping
down and raking the fish which abounded here in
myriads.*

19 November
Left Capetown enroute for Durban.

4

20–23 November
The sea was a little choppy and the ship rolled to a very heavy swell which is very frequent round the coast of South Africa, one or two of our fellows being sick – the first time since we left Southampton.

Arrived in Durban about 8 at night (23 November) and lay out in the Offing all night being visited by a detachment from the Warship HMS Terrible *which lay here.*

24 November
Disembarked when we were met by some very kind ladies and gentlemen who gave us bread, bananas and tobacco and even went so far as to write letters and addresses and send money home for any of us who wanted to send it away and when it arrived home there was generally more money in that what we gave them. We entrained for Nottingham Road station in open cattle trucks arriving later on at Pietermaritzburg where we left the Storemen of Companies and our kit, taking only with us one change of under linen. Here the ladies were very kind to us giving us papers, cakes, sandwiches, tobacco and clay pipes and after dining off potatoes and bully beef we departed singing 'Soldiers of the Queen' arriving at Nottingham Road station at dusk. I may mention here that all the way up the line we were treated very well by the ladies at the small stations we stopped at, miniature Union Jacks being displayed at intervals all along the line, we trying to repay the ladies for their kindness by giving them our badges which they prized very much.

Chambers recorded that *'later on in the war when our Regiment took Vaal Krantz, our cap badges were in great demand, the inhabitants of Natal paying 5 shillings for one, a rather high price for them when one gets them out of stores by paying one penny each, so much was the Regiment thought of.'*

We detrained at Nottingham Road station and marched to the camping ground where we stood and got drenched to the skin when we pitched our tents. I was then turned out on Outpost Duty all night.

Later, looking back, Private Chambers felt *'that that first night in the country was the most miserable one I ever had all through the War. I have had worse yet I was more used to them and did not think so much of it.'*

A terrible thunderstorm came in the like I had never before experienced though very common in South Africa as I later found out in that country.

25 November
Stopped in camp all day.

26 November–1 December
Entrained to Mooi River where we camped doing Outpost Duty on the surrounding hills. Remained here while our Brigade formed up namely the famous Light Brigade consisting of the Rifle Brigade [1st Rifle Brigade], *2nd*

Scottish Rifles [Cameronians], *Kings Royal Rifle Corps
and the* [1st Battalion] *Durham Light Infantry, the only
red coated*[1] *Regiment in the Brigade. The Boers in the
meantime being at Frere.*

*2 December
Marched to Willow Grange and encamped for the night
learning that the Boers had blown the railway bridge up
and left.*

*3 December
Marched to Estcourt and camped for one night.*

*4 December
Marched to Frere a distance of 14 miles and we were all
done up when we got there, the heat being terrific and the
roads knee deep in dust.*

*5 December
We had a days rest which was very welcome not having
got used to the road and country yet.*

*6 December
I visited the armoured train, where Winston Churchill
was taken prisoner,*[2] *which was watched by the Boers,
also the graves of the poor fellows who fell while defending*

---

1 The red coat, as a field uniform was last worn in action in the late 1880s.
2 WSC was a war correspondent for the *Morning Post* and whilst travelling from Escourt
to Chievely on 19 November 1899 the train was ambushed by the Boers. WSC became a
prisoner of war but escaped on 12 December 1899.

it. A temporary bridge was being erected in place of the other one which had been blown up.

General Buller decided to split his force into three for an advance into the Orange Free State but suffered three setbacks. There were defeats at both Stormberg (10 December) and Magersfontein (11 December). The third setback was to take place four days later at Colenso, thus completing the so-called Black Week.

7–11 December
Very active in camp getting ready for a big battle also a big convoy for Ladysmith which we hope to relieve very shortly.

12–14 December
Marched to Chieveley where we camped for 3 days right in front of the enemies position, the strength of our force amounting to 23,000 all told. We did Outpost here till 13th of December our naval guns meantime shelling the Boers positions.

The Battle of Colenso

15 December
At 2.30am we struck camp and advanced towards the Boers positions, a long range of precipitous mountains, the river Tugela running directly underneath them and so

8

dividing us from the enemy. At day break our guns opened fire on the Boers positions Gen. Harts' Brigade,[1] The Irish Brigade, were to form the firing line while Gen Lyttleton's Brigade, namely my brigade were his supports. The firing line advanced up to the rivers edge and opened fire, the Boers not replying to our fireshells. We arrive at the waters edge when they opened a terrible fire, a variable hailstorm scattering our fellows like chaffe before a whirlwind. The Dublins tried to cross the river but the river is noted for its swift currents and is very deep. The enemy had also laid barbed wire in its bed. The consequence, they got entangled in the wire and were shot down whilst trying to extricate themselves and sank to the bottom owing to the weight of their ammunition and equipment. The heat was terrible and for ten hours we lay out in the open midst shot and shell and not a drain of water; finding the position impregnable we retired losing a Battery of Artillery though our fellows tried hard to recover them, Lord Roberts'[2] only son (Lt. Hon FHS Roberts K.R.R.C.) being shot dead whilst bravely attempting to recover them. The loss of our guns was caused through getting in rifle range of the enemy, a strong force of them having been secreted in ambush 1,000 yards in front of their positions, the consequence was they shot all the horses down making it impossible to remove the guns. We therefore retired back to Chieveley our losses amounting to something like 1,147 killed and wounded. The first of a series of British disasters.

---

1 Major General Arthur Fitzroy Hart.
2 Frederick Sleigh Roberts, 1st Earl (1832–1914), Supreme Commander in South Africa.

(News of the setbacks at Stormberg and Magersfontein had obviously not filtered through.)

Following these setbacks the British Government's first step was to appoint Lord Roberts at the age of sixty-seven as Supreme Commander in South Africa. The desperate need for more men was solved by sending out Militia companies and also by allowing the Volunteers to go out. The latter were previously precluded by Act of Parliament from serving overseas. Further sources of manpower were the Dominions: Australia and Canada.

16 December
Our Brigade and the Irish Brigade retired back to Frere where we camped till the 10th January.

19 December
We started the old routine – parade every morning and Outpost Duty in the evening.

Christmas Day

25 December
Being Xmas Day we enjoyed ourselves best we could under the circumstances and proceeded to open air service at 6.30am and at 8am we had our breakfast consisting of bacon, bread and coffee and after that we had different games such as football, rounders etc. The British Soldier

never letting any trouble however great deter him from his love of sport.

At 1pm we had our Xmas dinner consisting of stew and Xmas pudding though we could not find the currants the cook having either gambled them away or been playing at marbles and lost them.

Nevertheless it was as good as could be expected under such circumstances.

At 4.30pm tea. The old usual bread and bread, then we sat and lit our pipes spinning yarns as only a soldier or sailor can till 8.30pm when we retired into a blanket and the hard veldts. So ended Christmas Day 1899 the likes of which I never wish to see again when thinking of the dark clouds that lay over our beloved country at that time, the country we had so willingly left to fight her troubles in a far off land and to uphold the Honour of Old England name.

26 December
Bank Holiday which is never recognised by the army, we resume our every day duties.

Chapter II

1900

1 January
New Years Day which brought something good in the
shape of plum pudding from Lyons & Co., London also
tobacco from Salmon and Glucksteins for which we were
very grateful and we thank the Donors very much.

Lord Roberts, together with Lord Kitchener who had been appointed to be his Chief of Staff, arrived at Cape Town, South Africa on board *Dunnottar Castle* on 10 January.

One of the first tasks identified was to build up the military strength but Lord Roberts was prepared to remain on the defensive until he was ready. Apart from improving railway communications, they collected a vast number of oxen, mules and wagons, giving each regiment its own train. Raising the personal hygiene standard of his troops was also of paramount importance and the soldiers had to be made to overcome the problem of dealing with an enemy who shot at him but was seldom seen. Most of the Boers had been bred to the horse and rifle and had seen commando service against Africans. Expert horsemen and marksmen, they could live off the country. Within a month, Roberts felt that he was ready to take the offensive.

Kimberley was relieved on 16 February and after his victory in the ten-day battle at Paardeberg he pushed on seizing the capital of the Orange Free State, Bloemfontein, on 13 March. Part of Lord Roberts' strategy had been to entice Boer reinforcements away from Natal in support of the Boer General, Pier Cronje, with the object of reducing resistance to the progress of General Buller in Natal.

In the meantime General Buller was responsible for the drive forward in the east towards Ladysmith and was quoted as saying 'We are going to the relief of our comrades in Ladysmith, and there will be no turning back.'

The great obstacle in the way of Buller's advance, however, was the strong Boer outpost on Spion Kop. The Kop was the topmost point of a plateau whose average height was 4,500 feet, five or six miles long and about three miles wide. Sir Charles Warren[1] was charged with capturing this position.

---

1 Sir Charles Warren (1840–1927) commanded 5th Division in South Africa.

10 January
Now our hardships begin. We marched to Springfield fording rivers and dongas[1] the rain drenching us to the the skin.

11 January
Marched to Spearmans Hill and camped there till the 19th of January.

19 January
Marched over Spearmans Hill opposite our Brigade getting under fire, two men of the King's Royal Rifles being killed and several wounded; eventually we arrived at Potgieters Drift under Mount Alice, half our Regiment being escort to the guns, the remaining half holding a small kopje[2] on the bank of the Tugela where we stayed for four days. Our guns, meanwhile were shelling the Boers positions namely Spion Kop, Ladysmith Rd. I may state that during this halt of four days an episode occurred which was nearly the means of ending this diary for ever. I went bathing one day and got in the swift current of the river and could not get out again. Fortunately for me there were some more fellows in the river and by the combined efforts of 4 of them I was got out safely to land, not much the worse for an adventure which very nearly ended my existence by drowning at a place which in time after became the grave of many of our gallant fellows.

---

1 Gully made by soil erosion.
2 A low hill.

The positions of General Buller's troops were such that General Barton,[1] with 4–5,000 men, was on the right wing at Chieveley; General Lyttleton was in the centre, in front of Potgieter's Drift with another 4–5,000 men with General Warren occupying the Spion Kop plateau with 12–15,000 troops.

23–25 January
We started a general attack on Spion Kop crossing the Tugela on the enemy's pontoon and occupied a ridge of low lying kopjes which we named Maconochie Kopjes owing to having Maconochie rations[2] nearly all the time we lay in them. We made a reconnaissance in force on the right of Spion Kop the object being to draw the Boers on to us and allow Chas. Warren who was on the left to get through. Two regiments of our brigade made a frontal attack on Spion Kop and when in rifle range were subjected to a fearful fire, Officers and men falling fast – our casualties exceeding one thousand. We evacuated the hill through a mistake.

Early in February it was reported back in England that their 'jubilation last week at the result of the attack on Spion Kop received a rude shock almost as soon as it was written'. The commentary then referred to the withdrawal being 'splendidly

---

1 Geoffrey Barton (1844–1923) Major General Commanding Fusilier Brigade in South Africa.
2 Tinned meat and vegetable stew.

conducted'. Besides the fighting, however, 'the gallantry of which was taken for granted, the total effect seemed not so unsatisfactory as it first looked'. General Buller, with a splendid moral courage which gave him strength to neglect his words, 'there will be no turning back', had by his prompt retirement saved a wing of his army from a grave disaster. Relief of Ladysmith was anticipated in the following fortnight. It was further recorded that 'the relief of that unfortunate garrison seemed to be more a point of honour for the British Army in South Africa, as the effort becomes more difficult and the hope less keen.'

26 January
We are still guarding the ferry at Potgieters Drift and all is very quiet our guns have ceased firing and we are having a rest.

27 January
We had another sleepless night. The rain came down all night and we had to walk about all night blankets and topcoats being the other side of the river.

28 January
Raining hard all day.

29 January
Turned out a lovely day but awfully hot. We got fresh

meat and potatoes which was quite a change after living on bully beef and preserved vegetables for so long.

30 January
Our blankets and topcoats and waterproof sheets came over which were very acceptable.

31 January
We got paid 15/- (fifteen shillings)[1] per man – rather an unusual proceeding.

1 February
We received tobacco pipes and cigarettes from the residents of Durham and Northumberland, also some socks from the principal towns in the North of England for which we thank them very much.

2 February
Our gunners saw some Boers walking along their trenches and fired and soon dispersed them.

3 February
We retired back over Potgieters Drift and bivouacked opposite Vaal Krantz.

4 February
Stayed here all day, my section having to guard a farm which was occupied by loyal Boers.

---

1 Equivalent to 75 pence.

The Battle of Vaal Krantz

5 February
When the Durham Light Infantry gained a good name in the campaign. We started to shell the Boer positions with 72 guns consisting of 5in GA 4.7 Naval guns, Howitzers and other guns. At 7am the Infantry advanced to the edge of the rivers bank where we halted till 12am while the engineers were erecting a pontoon bridge across the river, the Boers, meanwhile shelling them with pom-poms and maxims wounding 12 of them. At 12.30 Colonel Woodland,[1] commanding the Durham Light Infantry received orders to take a hill on the left of the Ladysmith road called Vaal Krantz. At 2pm my Company, the advanced Company of the Regiment advanced on to the pontoon bridge, the Boers keeping a very hot pom-pom fire and maxim fire on it, so we had to run for it one at a time till all had crossed over. As it was impossible to advance on top of the river bank we crept along under the rivers edge until we came in line with that part of the ridge called Vaal Krantz which we had to take. Our Company Officer gave us the order to get on top of the rivers bank and no sooner had we done so when the bullets flew around us in thousands. Of course we lay flat on our stomachs for there was not the smallest particle of covering to be got – we were on an open plain and we had the plain to cross through a mealie[2] field before we

---

1 Col. A.L. Woodland, C.B.
2 Maize: corn cob.

18

reached the foot of the hill. Our Company Officer gave the order to advance but they were the last words he uttered for he got two bullets through the neck killing him instantly (Major J. Smyth) and now begins deaths struggle first through a donga then tripping over barbed wire dodging through the mealies one minute, flat on your back the next minute careering for sheer life; shells and bullets flying in all directions, a man dropping here and another there but it is every man for himself; now we get among some rocks, now flat behind a rock then up again and rushing for another rock a few yards ahead. Then we reach the foot of the hill breathless but still full of hope, when we get the order to fix bayonets and now begin the struggle up, up we climbed. One sees a comrade fall shot through the head, another falls dashing his brains out on the rocks below still up we go with a British cheer midst mauser bullet and pom pom shell while Long Tom[1] on Doornkloof keeps dropping those 90lbs shells amongst us. Still up we go bereft of all feeling except one desire to reach the top of the hill. Death or Victory it is and now at last we have accomplished our object and at last we are on the top of the hill to find the Boers have fled except a few who have been too late and who hold up their hands when they see us only to drop them again and fire on us. I saw one of our fellows catching the Boer picking up his rifle again, rushed up to him, the look of madness in his eyes, eyes half starting from their sockets so intense was the moment, throw his rifle over his shoulder, the next moment to bring it down with terrible force on to the head

---

1 Nickname for one of the Boers new heavy guns by Creusot; 30 feet long firing 6in shells.

of the luckless Boer, smashing it to a pulp – so perish all treachery. Here Lieut. CD Shafto, poor fellow, whilst bandaging the wrist of Lieut. RR Lambton[1] who had been shot there received a pom-pom shell in the shoulder killing him instantly. The dusk coming on quickly for you have no twilight in South Africa, we started to entrench ourselves for the night tired out yet dare not sleep, the Boers endeavouring to take the hill again. False hope.

They did not know what Tommy is made of though they have learnt since. Our losses that day, I mean my Regiment, 2 Officers and 10 men killed and over 100 wounded.

It was reported in the weekly publication *Black and White Budget* on 24 February 1900 that 'The advance on Monday, February 5th was admirably carried out, the chief features being the heroism of the Durhams and the splendid charge of the Rifle Brigade on Vaal Kranz.'

6 February
We lay on the hill all day, the Boers attacking the hill on the left in the afternoon about 3.15. Again we drove them off, our 2nd in Command, Lt. Col. FitzGerald getting shot in the chest just above the heart. They managed to get up the hill with a biscuit per man and a tin of bully beef between 10 men, we had to pass the biscuit along the

---

1 Lambton was the first descendant of General John Lambton, who raised the Regiment in 1758, to serve in the Durham Light Infantry. He was later killed on the slopes of Drakensberg.

*trench on our stomach – to raise your head meant a bullet
through it. One poor fellow chanced it only to receive a
bullet through the forehead killing him instantly. This is
the time when you think of the evil you have committed
in your past. I have seen men praying, I have seen private
soldiers take the part of a clergyman over the grave of a
comrade and I may tell you I offered up a prayer praying
I may get up the hill safely – it was a proper death trap,
we were being fired at from 3 different directions. At 6pm
Gen Hildyards[1] Brigade relieved us on the hill and we
retired at dusk having been on the hill 26 hours and had
one biscuit. I may mention that during this morning 16th
Company RGA dropped a shell into the Boers magazine
exploding it and killing many Boers. We could see them
going in the air in pieces.*

7 February
*We had bivouacked under Mount Alice the night previous
and this morning the enemy dropped their 'Long Tom'
shells amongst us all day starting at breakfast. One shell
dropped in the first companies rifles which were piled,
shaking the whole Battalions rifles down and making a
hole deep enough to bury a horse. We were shelled all day
but received no casualties.*

8 February
*We retired back to Chieveley doing it in three days and
landed in on Sunday the 11th when after I had been in*

---

1 Henry John Thornton Hildyard (1846–1916) commanded 5th Division in South Africa
– General and KCB 1900.

camp half an hour, I fainted through the heat of the sun
and was convalascent for two days, the two days we rested
at Chieveley.

In furtherance of achieving the relief of Ladysmith, Gen. Hildyards' Brigade assaulted and took the southern end of Monte Cristo (see below) while the Royal Welsh Fusiliers and the rest of the Brigade assaulted the enemy on the eastern flank.

Monte Cristo

14–18 February
We advanced on Monte Cristo taking the enemy
completely by surprise who did not expect us coming that
day, it being Sunday. They fled leaving everything and
we availed ourselves of clothes they left in flight, blankets,
mackintoshes, books etc. There were even dinners cooking
on their fires. Of course we ate them as the Boers had got
flour, potatoes, bread rusks and all manner of things. We
also found wounded Boers, dead horses and plenty of
ammunition and by the amount of womens clothes it
showed they had their women with them.

Owing to the illness of Lieutenant General Sir C.F. Clery, Colonel Norcott was now in command of the 4th Brigade, and Major General Lyttleton of the 2nd Division.

19 February
Rested for the day which we made good use of. Rained
very hard all day and was wet and miserable.

20 February
We got the order to take Green Hill which we advanced
and took, the Boers having fled across the other side of the
river. We retired to the hill and remained there for three
days being sniped at every time we went for a drop of
water which was 3 miles off and then only being able to
get about an egg cup full at a time – so scarce was water.
We had one casualty those 3 days.

24 February
We marched to Fort Wiley just above Colenso, Bartons
brigade having occupied Colenso [on 19 February].

A final attack on the Boers positions by General
Buller before reaching Ladysmith resulted in
capturing Pieter's Hill. This was approached by a
precipitous ascent of 500 feet up which General
Buller led the gallant Dublin Fusiliers and two
battalions of the 6th Brigade.

Battle of Pieter's Hill

25 February
We advanced to Grobelaars Kloof[1] where we were
reserves to the Irish Brigade who had to take a hill called
Railway Hill on the left of Pieter's Hill.

They lost a fearful lot of men, the Inniskilling Fusiliers
being completely cut up. They retired off the hill and the
Durham Light Infantry were ordered to relieve them and
when we went up our fellows got knocked over like nine-
pins. This was Saturday morning. On Sunday morning
both sides sued for an armistice and we buried 80 of all
Regiments – Colonels lying dead amongst the Privates.
All one rank in death now.

We retired off the hill before the armistice was over and
no sooner had we got to our bivouack, namely Eagles
Nest, than the Boers opened a terrific fire on us but
fortunately, owing to the darkness none was hit. I forgot to
mention that my Regiment was ordered to take the hill
again after the Irish Brigade had abandoned it. The
Boers tried to deceive us by blowing bugle calls and
shouting out 'Retire the Durhams' which resulted in some
of our fellows getting knocked over; it was pitch dark and
one could not see one's hands in front of you. The Boers lit
fires on the right and left of the hill and when our fellows
went by the light they were shot down. I was close by and

---

1 A mountain ravine.

24

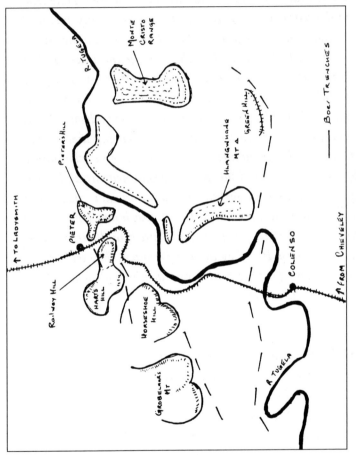

Battle of Pieter's Hill.

saw my comrades fall right and left and I made my way back from the fire as soon as possible. I must say Providence must have been at my side through that terrible ordeal. It was wonderful how I escaped. How true are the words here 'A thousand shall fall at thy side and ten thousand at thy feet yet thou shall remain untouched'. Never while I live do I wish to be in the likes of that again – it was a veritable death trap. We had to stop on the hill all night. The next morning the sight that met our eyes was horrible, our comrades lay in our midst dead and dying; some expired while we were carrying them down the hill to the ambulance van which, owing to the nature of the ground, could not get anywhere near us and when the armistice was agreed on we found more dead and dying comrades, men who but a few hours before were talking and jesting with us, now stark and stiff in their last long sleep. But they are not forgotten, they will live in our memory for they died heroes deaths and so ended the Battle of Pieter's Hill.

28 February
We got the order to be ready to advance in support to the Rifle Brigade who had to take Railway Hill again while Barton's Brigade were to occupy Pieter's Hill. Just before we started Sir Chas. Warren read out a telegram from Lord Roberts in which he stated he had, that morning, captured Cronje and his army and, as we knew we had opened the road to Ladysmith and soon expected to relieve that place, we were very cheerful and gave three hearty cheers which only British soldiers can give.

Whilst the capture of the Boer General was a tremendous boost to the morale of the British troops, the timing could be considered ironic as the 28th February was known as Majuba Day, the day when the Boers celebrated their 'Independence of 1881' regarding it as their victory over the British.

It was reported at the time that the surrender of General Cronje on the anniversary of Majuba Hill 'disposed at least of an annoyance which the British residents in the Transvaal had to put up with. Each anniversary was made a general holiday by the Transvaal Government and though English firms did not recognise it, Dutch firms employing British hands did, and consequently much ill feeling was aroused.' Cronje, with his wife, was to spend the rest of the war in St Helena, following in the footsteps of Napoleon.

The Relief of Ladysmith

Then we waited beside our arms while our guns shelled the enemy's position. I do not think there is any man living who heard the like of that afternoon before; the bombardment was something terrific. Then we advanced and took the hill under a very hot rifle fire. The pom-pom again proving itself a very useful thing in warfare, if only to make your flesh creep when you hear it. The Brigade on our right also succeeded in their plan and took about

50 prisoners. The stretcher bearers found 72 dead and wounded and there were even women in those trenches. The Boers had all retired leaving us masters of the situation and our Cavalry rode into Ladysmith to tell them they were relieved and their troubles were over.

Sir George White[1] rode out to meet them and ended the Siege of Ladysmith which must rank amongst the annals of British history as one of the finest pieces of work carried out through all the Campaign. Sir George White so gallantly held the town against overwhelming odds and looked after the inhabitants so well during that long incarnation and not forgetting the 'Relief Force' who, though forced to retire from impossible positions, never gave it up – three times they were forced to retire yet never gave in but still persisted on and the fourth time they accomplished the task they commenced four months before. Not in all the war do I think men suffered more than they did before Ladysmith was relieved, not merely because I was one of them but for pluck and endurance and after retiring three times they still stuck to the hard task manfully and I can safely say they could not be equalled. The Infantry, the despised footsoldier here showed to great advantage and they maintained or even proved themselves to be superior than the time when Napoleon the Great, who is considered the finest soldier the world has ever seen, said those famous words 'If I had English soldiers and French officers I could conquer the world.' Truly a great compliment from one so exalted.

---

1 George Stuart White (1835–1912) commanded Army in Natal 1899. Commanded Ladysmith Garrison 2 November 1899–1 March 1900.

I had the misfortune to walk into Ladysmith with my boots soled with biscuit tins held together by thongs strapped round the ankles made and cut from the skins of dead oxen we lost on the road, and I must confess I was footsore, together with the knees and seat of my pants minus, it was time we succeeded or we should soon have all been naked.

In his despatch of 10 March 1900 Winston Churchill, as correspondent for the *Morning Post,* commented that 'all through the morning into the afternoon the long stream of men and guns flowed through the streets of Ladysmith and all marvelled to see what manner of men these were dirty, war-worn, travel stained, tanned, their uniforms in tatters, their boots falling to pieces, their helmets dinted and broken.'

Verily it was what you might call soldiering in real earnest for we had slept on the open veldt for the last 6 weeks very often nothing but the half torn thin suit of khaki to keep us warm. Not for the wealth of a Rothchild would I go through that terrible ordeal again to experience the same again, though I thank 'Our Heavenly Father' I was so far spared where so many had fallen for the 'Honour of Old England's name'.

Lord Roberts' success at Paardeburg, with the capture of General Pier Cronje was partly instrumental in enabling the Relief of Ladysmith to come when it did. If men had not been drawn away from the trenches around Pieter's Hill, the task might have remained impossible, as Lord Roberts seemed to have considered it.

Winston Churchill described part of the advance with characteristic spirit. He did not know which to praise most, the advance of the British, or the defence of the Boer, but finally summed up in favour of the attack: 'If the defence was magnificent, the attack was superb.'

One of the great events after the relief of Ladysmith was reported at the time to have been the grand march past of Sir Redvers Buller's men before Sir George White.

For his efforts Private Chambers received a 'Relief of Ladysmith' clasp to go with his Queen's South Africa medal.

Coincidentally his future grandson's maternal grandfather was at Ladysmith during the siege serving with the 5th Royal Irish Lancers, and received a clasp for the 'Defence of Ladysmith.' Both sets of medals are now in the hands of their grandson.

1 March
We marched through Ladysmith and were guard of honour to General Sir Redvers Buller,[1] *'Our Hero' who*

---

1 S.P.G. Ward in *The History of the Durham Light Infantry* states that Buller did not enter Ladysmith until 3 March.

*through all the trials, difficulties and misfortunes of war
and the fate of England at stake, still held up his courage,
proved himself the leader of men and won for himself a
name only surpassed by the confidence his men reposed in
him all through that terrible struggle and fought under
him through all. I have seen him in the field at Aldershot.
I have waited by his side at dinner and I have seen him
when the fight has been at its height with shot and shell
bursting all around and, in all I have found him the
Brave and Courteous Soldier.*

It was widely known that Buller did not always
show great tact when dealing with his superiors or
equals but he was highly respected by his troops
despite the setbacks in the early part of the war. It
was reported that 'Buller inspired more personal
admiration and love than any other General of the
time; never once have his men lost faith in him and,
to keep the confidence of the rank and file, who
know nothing of a leader's plans, after repeated
reverses, is indeed a rare gift and one that cannot be
too highly valued.'

2 March
*We moved to Sundays river just by Elandslaagte a name
made famous by the gallant work done by the British
troops when they completely cut up the German Legion, a
mob of renegade Germans and showed the world what
Englishmen can do. Here we made a camp and stopped*

till the tenth of April enjoying the rest we so well deserved, our duties being chiefly composed of parades in the day and outpost at night.

Whilst at Sunday's River Major General Lyttleton was succeeded in the command of the 4th Brigade by Colonel C.D. Cooper.

3 March–10 April
We have just received the mail from home and enjoying a few blissful moments in reading of our Beloved ones at Home. We also received our Chocolate Box, a grateful present from Her Majesty Our Beloved Queen which when we think of that Beloved One would fight for Her to our very last. During our stay here we play the heats in our Regimental Football Cup Tie for Tommy Atkins never even allows war to stop his love of football and so with a little enjoyment and a bit of duty we pass our time away till the 10th April.

The chocolate boxes were designed by Messrs J.S. Fry and Sons of Bristol who sent out 40,000 of the whole number. The rest of the chocolate was manufactured by Messrs Cadbury and Rowntree. By the Queen's express desire only her soldiers would have the tins and orders were issued for the destruction of the dies when the required number had been manufactured.

One soldier wrote home saying 'I have forwarded it

*Private Chambers' Army New Testament inscribed
'South Africa 1900' and Chocolate Box.*

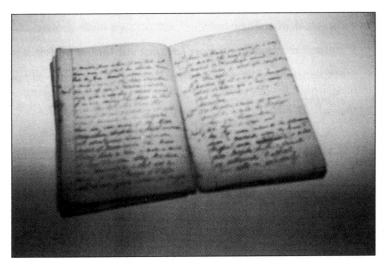

Private Chambers' Diary.

[the chocolate box] home just as I received it in order that you and the children may share as well as myself in a present from our gracious Queen. You ought to have been here when the chocolate was served out. You could hear the regiments cheering all round the camp. A lot more fellows are sending the present home. There are a good many men without friends at home, and those who have are trying to buy the box from them, but no one will part with so precious a souvenir, not even for £5. One chap told me he would carry it about with him, and it would have to wear his pocket out before he would part with it.'

The Shelling of Elandslaagte

10 April
We are on parade making a sham attack on a hill overlooking our camp when to our consternation we find it occupied by the Boers who, thinking we are attacking the hill in real earnest open fire on us with their Long Toms, which means us beating a hasty retreat not being aware the Boers were so close, their shells dropping amongst us with dreadful accuracy many poor fellows getting knocked over but after a short interval the Boers, meanwhile having all their own road, our naval guns got into position and quickly stopped their fire, a shell from one of our 4.7 guns hitting one of their guns which sent it up in the air and we had the satisfaction of seeing the

wheels alone coming down the hill, the mechanism of their gun being blown to atoms.

From this affair I pen the following account of the fight at Elandslaagte.

On the 10th April the Boers unexpectedly shelled the Durhams while on parade from which I quote the following:

> *They fired their guns – we heard the snap.*
> *They thought they'd got us in a trap*
> *Not a word among the men was said*
> *They knew it was CO's parade*
> *So they left it to him to bring them through*
> *For he would do it well they knew*
> *And that day there was little slaughter*
> *When he flanked the Boer at Elandslaagte*
> *They had their own way for a bit*
> *But very soon they had to flit*
> *Our lads in blue soon got the range*
> *And very soon there was a change*
> *Their pom-poms have a curious sound*
> *As near you, they come bobling round*
> *And their Mausers how they sweetly sing*
> *That little song entitled 'ping'*
> *Our lads in blue, our lads in red*
> *For England, streams of blood have shed*
> *Fighting morning, noon and night,*
> *That every one should have the right*
> *So when the War is fairly over*
> *And Tommy and Jack on English shore*
> *Let everyone give honour due*
> *For all our lads in red and blue.*

11 April
We pitched camp between two hills 3 miles from Elandslaagte station.

12 April
Remained all this day in camp.

13 April
We were all turned out at 2.30am and rolled our blankets, packed them on wagons and stood (to arms) as there was an alarm raised and we expected another attack. We waited till day light when we were dismissed not having learnt the cause of the alarm. I think it was a false one given by the Outposts.

14 April
Passed off without any unusual occurrence.

15 April
Being Easter Sunday we went to open air service at 7.30am when we listened to a very nice sermon.

16 April
Bank Holiday. We amused ourselves with pick and shovel building trenches and carrying big stones for fortifications. Thats how we spent Easter Monday, rather a different one from my last Easter holiday.

17 April
We arose at 3.30am, struck camp and at 6.30 marched

off and with some Artillery and the Kings Royal Rifles retired back to Modder Spruit and pitched camp.

18 April
The Regiment all turned out at 10am and started hay-making; rather an unusual proceeding on active service. So to keep us busy they made us get on our hands and knees and pick grass as it was so very long and veldt fires are so very prevalent and soon spread.

19 April
Making roads for water carts, digging stones and pulling long grass which lasted all day.

20 April
We had musketry practice at long range volleys and at night proceeded on outpost duty.

21 April
Heavy gun firing heard at Elandslaagte. We are to stand to arms any moment (by order). It afterwards proved to be the Boers shelling the Elandslaagte coal mines.

22 April
The SALH[1] were engaged by the Boers from the Biggarsberg and it is rumoured that 2 guns have been captured from the enemy.

---

1 South African Light Horse.

23 April
We received a consignment of woollen mufflers and socks
from the wife of Captain Parke of ours and a more
suitable thing could not have been sent as the winter is
coming on and the nights are intensely cold and we are
all extremely grateful for their kindness.

24 April–6 May
This morning was very cold and we are being served out
with another blanket each which will prove very
beneficial to us. We stay here till May 7th occupying the
time with building trenches and walls, outpost duty and
parades. During this stay I had a rather unpleasant
adventure which I will relate. One morning I was sitting
in the tent on my bed, the tent walls being raised as it was
very hot, writing home when I happened to glance at my
side only to see a snake gliding by my side. As soon as I
recovered myself sufficiently I made one jump and sprang
out of the tent. Wynter and I chased the snake and I put a
brush on its neck when it spat at us. Fortunately I got it
across the cheek but poor old Wynter got it full in the eyes
and for an hour he suffered untold agony. I really thought
he was blinded. The Doctor put something in his eyes and
so relieved some of the pain. Eventually we attracted its
attention while Doling went up behind it and with the
kitchen knife nearly severed its head from its body. It
proved to be a Puff Adder of a deadly species and
measured close on 4 feet. I thanked my stars it was dead.
Wynter skinned it and sent it home; a relic of one hours
untold agony and a startling adventure.

On 3 May Lord Roberts' central column started to push northwards towards Pretoria overcoming Kroonstad very quickly. By now he was impatient to end the war, although on the western flank Mafeking was still under siege. Roberts had originally wanted Buller to join him on the Vaal for a joint thrust on Pretoria. Buller, however, insisted on crossing the Biggarsberg and clearing the main railways northwards, taking his three divisions over the Natal passes and into the Transvaal up to Standerton.

7 May
8am we struck camp and at 1.30 we started to march to Lombard's Farm where they took our tents off us.

8 May
Stayed for the day and at night found it very cold without tents.

9 May
9am we moved off again forming a flying column of Cavalry, Artillery and Infantry when we marched 12 miles.

Between 10–15 May Buller outflanked several thousand Boers dug into the Biggarsberg, which was regarded by some as one of the neatest tactical feats of the war. He was to successfully repeat the exercise in early June when he outflanked a well-entrenched Boer force at Laing's Nek.

10 May
We halted for the day among a lot of trees and were joined
by General Clery[1] *and the remaining half of our brigade.*
I was very sick; 102 with fever.

11 May
Well as ever, we marched to Waschbank river and
bivouacked. We were rear guard and had to wait till all
the baggage had passed us arriving in camp at 1am. My
Company waggon broke down so had to sleep with
nothing on all night.

12 May
At 6am we marched another 15 miles. On this march we
had to run the gauntlet, the veldt being one mass of
flames and in some places we had to run through them.
Came very near blowing our ammunition waggon up by
the fire. Arrived in camp at 8pm and sent two companies
to our left at the foot of Biggarsberg.

The Flanking of Biggarsberg

13 May
Sunday morning. At day break the Boers shelled our
camp, one shell dropping within 3 yards of where I stood,
but fortunately for me buried itself in the ground without
explosion. We advanced and starts a race for first place,
the Boers or us for the position which we are trying to

---

1 Sir Cornelius Francis Clery (1838–1926) 2nd Division in South Africa.

take so has to turn their flank. We arrived a few minutes ahead when we opened fire on the Boers with our pom-pom the first time we have used them and so held the position and bivouacked on it for the night.

14 May
Marched on through Helpmakaar Pass, a terrible pass where if we had not have made the flank we should have had to face terrible odds. Very hot and dusty and signs of the Boer everywhere.

15 May
We set off again for Dundee and arrived safe after a very long and tedious march of 20 miles driving the Boers in front of us. They left the town that morning as we marched in at night closely pursued by our Cavalry. Here we saw traces of the Boers everywhere; sheepskins and filth scattered all about, every house showed signs of devastation, the Boers having lived in them and made a mess of everything. One thing I noticed most particularly and that was a photo of the Princess of Wales which was quite intact and not damaged a bit.

16 May
Here at Dundee we rested for a day and made the most of it.

17 May
Marched to Dannhauser about 13 miles and landed in about 3pm. Camped for the night.

Meanwhile on the western front the siege of Mafeking was over when Lt. Col. Herbert Plummer and Col. Bryan Mahon entered the city. Colonel Baden Powell (who founded the Scout movement) had defended Mafeking for six and a half months.

18 May
Marched off again at 6.15am for Newcastle, about 22 miles and after a very weary and hard day arrived at 6pm and bivouacked.

19 May
Our Brigade started off again and marched 12 miles to Ingogo where we bivouacked.

20 May
We had a days rest.

21 May
My Regiment were ordered to advance again and marched again to Mount Prospect under Inkiuela, 7 miles from Majuba Hill and formed an advanced Outpost. Very cold and winterly.

22 May
We are on Outpost watching the Boer positions at Majuba Hill, Laing's Nek and Pugwange.

23 May
No rations arrived for us so we had to go pretty short.

24 May
Caught two Boers. It being the Queen's birthday we all
fell in on parade and gave 3 hearty cheers with as much
heartiness as though we were on parade in Aldershot
instead of being under Majuba Hill and within range of
Boer guns.

25 May
On Outpost. Nothing unusual occurred.

26 May
English mail arrived when I got 3 letters and one paper.
Sent Ladysmith relief ribbons home.

27 May
All quiet. Outpost as usual.

28 May
We received the good news.[1] Mafeking relieved.

29 May
Our Brigade moved up to the foot of Inkquayla
Mountain when the Boers opened fire from Pugwange
dropping shrapnel at 5 miles range but were soon stopped
by our guns.

30 May
We were supplied with fresh meat, but still on hard biscuits.

---

1 This was the day when the British announced the annexation of the Orange Free State
and renamed it Orange River Colony.

31 May
Our guns shelled Majuba, Laing's Nek and Pugwange.

1 June
All is quiet. Very cold and windy.

2 June
We have just received the issue of winter clothing which are very acceptable and exchange our rags.

3 June
Rumour is going about that Lord Roberts is in Johannesburg and preparing to advance on Pretoria.

Roberts' central flank, under Lieutenant General Ian Hamilton, had crossed the river Vaal on 26 May and took Johannesburg on Thursday, 31 May. Meanwhile, President Kruger[1] left Pretoria on 29 May travelling east to Machadadorp and took most of the Transvaal Government with him. Entry into Pretoria took place on 2 June.

4 June
We have just received the Staff of Life once again and the line is expected to be in working order again in a few days time.

---

1 Stephanus Johannes Paulus Kruger (1825–1904), President of the Transvaal (1883–1900).

5–12 June
The remainder of our division are trying to effect an
entrance through Almonds Nek or Bothas Pass. We are
still doing Outpost duty and anxiously awaiting news of a
move or Roberts movements. We get the welcome news that
Lord Roberts has entered Pretoria.

The Evacuation of Laings Nek by the Boers and its Occupation by the British

12 June
Moved off at 2pm to march through Laings Nek, the
Boers having meanwhile evacuated those positions owing
to Bullers splendid achievement in forcing his way through
Bothas Pass which was one of the most brilliant moves
ever made in this campaign, when the Boers lit the grass
with the intention of attacking our fellows through the
cover of smoke. But here it seemed that Kruger's God had
neglected him for no sooner had the fire got a good hold on
the veldt than the wind changed round having been
blowing in the face of the British troops. Consequently it
blew in the face of the Boers who no sooner saw the
change, when they turned and scooted, our fellows doing
the charging, through the smoke, and so won the Pass
which enabled that force to make a flank and so come in
rear of the Boers at Volkrust and Charlestown and the
Boers not being prepared to be between the fire of our
Brigade and the other force, promptly decamped which

also enabled our Brigade to advance on to Laings Nek where we found most impregnable positions which, had we tried a frontal attack on them, would have resulted in our complete annihilation, there being tier upon tier of trenches enabling the Boers to have complete control of all the roads and front and pouring fire on us from three different heights and made it impossible to have captured that position. We marched through the Nek and bivouacked on the other side. Here we found the Boers Laager[1] with its motley group of tin hutches lately tenanted by the Boers, frying pan stoves, sheep skins, old tins, thousands of rounds of ammunition and filth all combined which go to making the Boer what we found out he was a dirty despicable, ignorant person. Farms and small houses and everything in the shape of such things, were utterly destroyed by the destructive enemy but left a piano,[2] beautifully toned instrument the sound of its sweet music in such an inopportune time brought back to me sweet memories of the old home in Dear Old England, never has she seemed more dearer to me than at that time in that lonely wrecked cottage on the slopes of Majuba Hill.

During the short stay here we spent a few happy hours in the society of that piano in the shape of a waltz and a smoking concert now and again.

---

1 An encampment.

2 It would appear that the Boers had a superstitious reverence for pianos. An extract from a letter from one of the Queen's Regiment was published in 1900 which said that 'there were a few houses there, near Chieveley, but they did not look up to much when the Boers had done with them. The Boers looted everything they could carry, but it is a strange fact that they won't touch a piano. We have come across a lot of houses, and the piano is about the only thing they have not broken.'

13 June
Our tents have arrived which we have not seen since the
7th of May. We have pitched our camp and intend to stay
for a few days in the meantime helping to clear Laings
Nek Tunnel which the Boers have blown up at each end.

14 June
Some 14 Boer prisoners were brought in, most English
and Irish renegades, a motley set of men.
Sharp frost at night and very cold indeed all through
the day.

15 June
I visited Majuba Hill and saw the graves of our
poor fellows who fell in 1881 from which I copied the
following:

In memory of Henry Brazier of
HMS Boadica who with 20 others
of the Naval Brigade were killed
near this spot Majuba Hill

Feb 27th 1881 – (aged 22).

In memory of one NCO and 29 Privates
of the 92nd Gordon Highlanders
who fell in action on the 27th Feb. 1881
and are here buried.
Gen Colley also fell near this spot.

On Laings Nek also reads the following:

**In memory of the
Hon Cornwallis Maude
only son of
Viscount Hawardin (aged 28)
who having resigned his commission
in the Grenadiers volunteered for
service while in South Africa and
being attached to the 58th Foot Reg.
(2nd Battalion Northamptonshire
Regiment) fell in action on Majuba
Mountain Feb 27th 1881.**

Another big grave stone had the following inscription:

In memory of their comrades who
were killed or died of their wounds
received in action at Majuba Hill on the
27th Feb 1881. Erected by the Officers
and men of the 58th Reg.

Capt. The Hon C Maude
Sergt T Kace
Corpl J Creagan   Corpl P Murray
Drummer Flannaghan
Privates   Addington
Andrews   Bloomfield
Bluff   Connors
Harmer   Gardiner
Pigneys   Collings
Guardon   Smith
Stone   Stone
Thompson   Longer
Trusswell   Vandy
Whitehouse   Williams
Williams   Grady
Seggans   Lovell
Mc Calhy   Court
Mc Ewan   Mc Iver
Mc Loughlin   Morrison
Osborne   Packer
Richardson   Richmond

We stayed at Laings Nek till the 19th of June.

19 June
We struck camp for another tour of marching, our destination being Standerton in the Transvaal. Passing through Charlestown we enter into the forbidden country, the country which we had waited so long to enter. We left Volkrust on our right, halted a few miles out of it and bivouacked for the night.

20 June
My birthday. Who ever thought I would spend it out here in this wilderness. We marched off again and marched a distance of 12 miles to a place called Zand Spruit where we halted for the night. A few Boers surrendered to us. On this march 1 caught my first glimpse of a Dutch Vrow, a young girl of about 18, not bad looking but very ugly shape, your Dutch women do not wear corsets which makes them look like a bag of oats tied in the middle.

21 June
We started off again for another 15 miles and arrived at a place called Paarde Kop and pitched camp for the night.

The British Entry into Standerton

22 June
We marched a distance of 23 miles; had our breakfast in
the road, namely, a biscuit and a piece of Bully Beef.
Marched again and halted for dinner. First course –
Bully Beef; Second course – dog biscuits. We left this halt,
namely a place called Platrand, and marched off again
and arrived into camp about 6 miles from Standerton
and halted for the night. I may mention that previous to
starting this days march we beheld, in the small hours of
the morning, a great light which in the darkness seemed
to be like some large town on fire. I thought of Moscow
and Napoleons hurried retreat and was sure the Boers
had burnt Standerton to the ground but I afterwards
found out that the light was the reflection from £1000
worth of railway sleepers which the Boers had set fire to.
These sleepers were what the Boers took out of Natal and
stocked them at Standerton for their own use never
thinking, I suppose, we should get that far into their
country but they did not know the British Soldier. Instead
of having a red coat and white helmet to fire at they had
men the colour of their beloved Veldt, men who in 9 short
months had learnt the Boer only too well and proved
themselves their equal in firing if not in treachery and
they found the accursed Rooinek[1] was one too much for
them and who taught them he was not one to be despised.

---

1 Afrikaan nickname for an Englishman.

23–29 June
At 10 am we set off for Standerton; arrived there quite
safe and pitched our camp to the left of the town
underneath a small ridge which I found out afterwards
was called Standerton Kop. We stayed at Standerton till
the 30th. During our short stay here I walked through the
town. In our country we should call it a village, but in the
Transvaal it is classed as a large town and is a very
important one for, being in the centre it gives easy access
to the small places in the Orange Free State and other
side to Bethal and Ermelo and numerous small places. It
also stands out in British importance for here the British
small force were besieged for 72 days in 1881 which was
only ceased by the Treaty of Peace which was signed in
O'Neill's farm at Laings Nek. A traitor in 1881 and we
found him the same when we marched through and so
banished him from home.

29 June
We get the order to strike camp and pack our wagons
which we did and then received the order to pitch camp
again.
  Lt Col Fitzgerald joined here having been home after
being severely wounded at Vaal Krantz on the 6th
February 1900. He appears to be well and strong again.

30 June
We struck camp again and this time we did march off at
9am a distance of some 12 miles or more to a place called

Vaal Laaghe where we arrived about 1.30 after a very trying and tedious march (I suppose we felt it more because we had been idling for 7 days). We bivouacked for the night, my Company going on Outpost.

1 July
At 9am we marched off again and came into contact with some stray Boers.

2 July
We set off on another wild Boer hunt and marched into a place called Greylingstad – here I saw my first gold mine.

3 July
Stayed here all day, some of our fellows visiting the gold mine.

Units of Buller's and Robert's armies first met on 4 July thereby transforming Roberts' supply situation by the linking of the Natal railway with Pretoria.

4–9 July
We marched off again for a place called Vlakfontein, 14 miles off, where we arrived about 5 o'clock having had dinner on the way. Our rear-guard were sniped all along the march by the Boers and traces of Boer handiwork were noticeable here, for the railroad was torn up for 2 miles, sleepers standing up on ones end and made them appear like a row of palisades. We stayed here for 5 days

when, during that period, we had to send for a convoy from Greylingstad as the line was not mended. We received the convoy just outside Greylingstad – started for Vlakfontein when we were attacked by 500 Boers who brought a big gun into the open, the first time I had seen them do such a thing, for the Boer likes to fight on a hill and have his enemy below him. However we drove them off, our side receiving 3 casualties and got safe in Vlakfontein again. While we were here Gen. Buller also marched through on his way to Pretoria to meet Lord Roberts. It was here also, we joined hands with Lord Roberts force and so established the line of communication between Capetown via Pretoria to Durban.

10 July
Having repaired the line and established communication with Lord Roberts we struck camp and marched back to Greylingstad and pitched camp when we received orders to be ready to march off again next morning for a four days march.

On return to Greylingstad and, until the end of September, the battalion formed part of a column under Lieutenant General Sir C.F. Clery which was continually on the move in the district of Greylingstad and Standerton.

11 July–15 August
When we marched off again for a 4 days march which

became a 15 days march, our destination no-where but chasing the Boers from one place to another, a rather silly game on our part I fancy, a foot soldier trying to catch a mounted one. We patrolled the country backwards and forwards from Standerton to Vlakfontein. We captured, including surrendered Boers, 350 which was chiefly the Standerton and Heidelberg commandos including Field Cornet Boshoff.

16 August
We arrived at Greylingstad and once more pitched our camp where we received a fresh diet, namely fresh meat and bread which came to us as a luxury for we had been on short rations, sometimes only receiving 2 biscuits per day, not much to march and fight on which we had done for the past 6 weeks.

17 August
When Gen. Clery broke our brigade up which had fought so well together for 10 months. The Scottish Rifles were sent on a hill right opposite the station.

18 August
The Rifle Brigade and Kings Royal Rifles and all the Staff went to Heidelberg while our Regiment guarded the line at Greylingstad.

19 August
Kit inspection. Outpost at night.

20 August
Our Colonel took us out for a march to several of the farms around Greylingstad and Waterval.

21 August
We struck camp and marched to Grange Farm a little to the left and front of Vlakfontein Station.

22 August
We had a reconnaissance under Gen. Clery towards Eden Kop but found out the Boers had left the night before.

23 August
We marched back to Greylingstad again in fearful windy weather which blew the dust along like a sandstorm and made us like a lot of niggers. We pitched camp again on the old ground.

24–28 August
We stayed here until the 28th during which time we had our sports. Miller won the obstacle race and Lesiter who I had watched only 12 months ago run for the Army Championship at Aldershot, won the 100 yards foot race. I never thought when I saw him at Aldershot I should so soon see him so far away.

Verily one never knows what will happen in this world. We struck camp and started to march to Standerton. We halted for the night at Waterval.

29 August–6 September
We were all up at 7am and was just going to strike camp when a terrific thunderstorm broke over us, rain coming down in torrents, so we received orders to standby and not strike camp. At 8.30 it cleared off so we struck camp and marched off to Standerton arriving there at 3pm doing 35 miles in 2 days. We stopped at Standerton till the 7th September doing outpost guarding the town etc.

Colonel Woodland of the Durham Light Infantry was invalided on 31 August 1900 and command was handed over to Lieutenant Colonel H.S. FitzGerald.

7–24 September
We marched off on the trek with Gen. Clery, chasing Boers, burning farms etc. for 18 days.

On 10 September Roberts annexed the Transvaal.

25 September –31 December
When we marched back into Standerton and then the Regiment broke up and 6 Companies went to guard 6 different approaches to the town and was stationed there, our duty to guard the town and send patrols at night to guard the lines.
On Christmas Day we had our Regimental sports and the Soldiers Home gave a tea to Tommy Atkins and tried to make us spend that day as happy as we could under the circumstances. I shall remember Xmas Day as I had

a gentle reminder having occasion to go to Standerton Kop in the buggy or Cape cart we had took from the Boers. I was coming down the hill when the mules skidded into the side of the hill throwing me head first on the other side. Lucky escape. I was only momentarily stunned. When I recovered I found the Officer M Bowers (who was riding with me) being dragged down the hill under the cart so when I got my senses I rescued him. It was rather laughable for the Officer had only just been remarking how lucky he was smoking a cigar and riding down to the station and then the next minute to find himself under a cart being dragged down the hill. I was very sorry afterwards for he is a nice officer and he had hurt his knees and torn his trousers. I think he had to go into hospital for a fortnight.

Boxing night I got a night off and Corporal Howe and myself proceeded to the station refreshment room where we dined and as we had not had the chance before we made a night of it – we had 2 bottles of Pomery and Greno rather expensive 17/6 [87¹/₂p] a bottle. Our dinner cost £2.1s.6d [£2.07¹/₂p] but we did not mind – we had enjoyed ourselves. We both had lunch there several times during the Xmas week.

In the meantime Buller had left South Africa at the end of October and received a hero's welcome back in Britain, at least from the crowds. Unlike Roberts, who was to receive an earldom and a substantial amount of cash, Buller was given no official honour.

Towards the end of the year there were conflicting views amongst the British generals as to the state of the War. Whilst Roberts claimed that the conflict was nearly over, others claimed that a disaster was imminent unless a more systematic military strategy was put in place.

The last eighteen months of the War were to turn into a bitter guerrilla affair with a series of commando raids being carried out by the Boers whilst the British tried to trap them into surrender. The last phase of the War continued for so long partly as a result of the lack of sufficient British mounted troops after most of the Yeomanry and colonial troops were sent home. Lord Kitchener, who had taken over from Roberts, eventually managed to obtain more mounted troops. By this time the total strength of the British Army in South Africa had risen to 260,000 against less than 20,000 Boers still fighting.

On 26 November 1900 Thomas Chambers was appointed Unpaid Lance Corporal.

Officers inspecting Outpost of 1st Durham Light Infantry at Eden Kop (from an original photograph in the diary).

Chapter III

1901

1 January
Began another year of misery for it is nothing more. One would feel twice as happy if one was fighting instead of sticking in one place, the same thing over and over again.

We entrained at Standerton, our first time in a train since Mooi River and proceeded to take up our quarters 50 miles from Standerton and 22 from Heidelberg, 3 miles from the line on a hill called Eden Kop, where in the midst of danger we are residing. When we get off I do not know. Our duty comprises Outpost Duty patrolling the line, laying on Kopjes trying to catch the Boers crossing over. Awaiting the call to either England or India which it is we don't know. But roll on.

From this point in the diary the recordings are less continuous, many periods/days not being accounted for. This may well be a reflection on the way the War was changing from one of major campaigns to guerrilla warfare and obviously Chambers' own involvement in such activities.

Sir Alfred Milner, High Commissioner for South

Africa and Governor of Cape Colony, was effectively civilian administrator of the Transvaal and the Orange Free Colony at this time, following the annexation of the two states by Roberts. He was to be influential over the coming months with the British Government and in particular with attempts to gain peace but not, unlike Kitchener, at any cost. His rift with Kitchener was very apparent.

Living off the land and organized in small mobile commandos, the Boers seized British supplies, cut rail tracks, overwhelmed small British units and eroded the fringe of larger columns. To crush the resistance Lord Kitchener adopted the 'scorched earth' policy, burning the Boers crops and destroying 30,000 farmsteads. Controversially, he also began to intern Boer families in concentration camps. Bad siting and poor medical facilities were to result in a mortality rate of up to 60 per cent in some camps and produced an outcry both in Britain and elsewhere.

20 April
Appointed Paid Lance Corporal.

10 June
I went to Heidelberg and had 13 teeth drawn out – very painful.

20 June
I am 25 today and during that period I have not known
12 months happiness in the whole time.

(Chambers was actually 26 years old in 1901. When he joined the Army in 1894 his age was incorrectly stated as 18 years 4 months. However, his birth certificate confirms his date of birth as 20 June 1875.)

22 June
Lieut Rasbotham and mounted Infantry went out and came in contact with the enemy killing one and wounding 3. Our loss was Lieut. Rasbotham killed and 2 men wounded.

23 June
Buried Lieut Rasbotham in the kirkyard at Hakfontein Station.

10 August
Lord Kitchener issued Proclamation confiscating all property and proclaiming after the 15th Sept all Rebels and to banish all Generals etc from the Country.

Boer prisoners were sent to the island of St Helena, a British possession but, as numbers increased, others were sent to Ceylon (now Sri Lanka), India and Bermuda.

7 September–19 October
Headquarters and 300 men proceeded to Heidelberg. The
remainder stayed guarding the line.

20 October
I have 7 years service today and have had quite enough
soldiering, though I guess I will have to do more.

Under the terms of Chambers' enlistment in the
Army he had signed on for *'7 years with the Colors,*
and 5 years in the Reserve or, if the man completes his 7
years' service while beyond the seas, then for 8 years with
the Colors and 4 years in the Reserve'.

21 October
When I reported sick and was admitted into hospital
suffering from debility caused through my teeth.

22 October
In hospital. My first time during my service.

23 October
Sent to convalescent depot.

24 October–14 December
Inspected by the doctor and had my name put on the
book to go before a Board to pass as an invalid for
England. May it pass alright and I shall be happy.
    For the last 6 weeks I have been staying here in

Convalescent Camp, permanent Orderly Sergeant and Orderly man as far as that goes. If I could only eat hard food I would much prefer to be with my comrades on the Veldt. As it is, I am not much use out there.

2 Years Anniversary of Colenso

15 December
It is now 2 years today since I trod on my first battle field, namely the Battle of Colenso and still we are on the same game. One would never have thought we should be doing the same as we were 2 years ago namely hunting the Boer. Pray heaven it will soon be over. What a dreadful 2 years have elapsed since that fateful 15 Dec. 1899 when it seemed if England had at last found her master. Yet God has been good and again England stands today unequalled in her glory and prosperity though many have paid dearly for it and today thousands of her best blood has been shed to uphold her standard.

By the flag they have battled for so long,
By the fame they have suffered so to save,
Honour be and praise to the gallant and the strong,
Honour to the bravest of the brave.

Let us hope that the day is not far distant when Boer and Briton shall clasp hand in hand and become brothers side by side in peace.

MY FIRST GLIMPSE OF A BOER FUNERAL

This afternoon I walked out my usual walk since I came into this camp, namely to the Boer Kirkyard and there Boer and Briton with head unbared stood side by side to witness the burial of a Boer child. What a strange world we live in; not many miles from here Boer and Briton are trying there uttermost to take each others life while here in that corner of God's acre Briton joins with Boer in sympathy for a loss he has just sustained – how true are those words 'God moves in a mysterious way'.

19 December
When the Doctor marked me for my Regiment.

20 December
When I left the convalescent camp for the detail camp.

21 December
When I left the town of Standerton enroute for Middelberg; arrived at Heidelberg at 8pm, Elandsfontein at 10pm where we changed for Pretoria. Arrived at Pretoria at 12pm where I had a cup of tea and lay on Pretoria station all night. Rained very hard.

22 December
Sunday. Went out at 7am, paid 2/- and had a good breakfast, the tea being the best I had had in the country. Walked out in Pretoria, enjoyed it immensely. 9.30 book train for Middelberg arriving there at 7pm. Took my kit

up to the Reg. Bought my tea and lay down. Stopped at the station all night.

23 December
Joined Headquarters for duty and was attached to H Company.

24 December
Took a good view of my future home for a bit went and heard the band of the 18th Hussars in the Market Square. My first Guard in the Regiment – just my luck mounted Guard Christmas Eve.

25 December
On Guard all day – miserable day. Had plum pudding for dinner. Dismounted Guard 6pm. Went with friend and spent rather a pleasant evening singing and had a drop of beer – returned home at 12pm.

26 December
Started the round of duty, guards and fatigues.

Duplicate

SHORT SERVICE.

(7 years with the Colors, and 5 years in the Reserve, or, if the man completes his 7 years' service
while beyond the seas, then for 8 years with the Colors and 4 years in the Reserve.)

ATTESTATION OF

No. *5319* Name *Thomas Chambers* Corps *Durham Lt. Infy*

Questions to be put to the Recruit before enlistment.

1. What is your Name?	1. *Thomas Chambers*
2. In or near what Parish or Town were you born?	2. In the Parish of *New George* near the Town of *Stafford* in the County of *Staffordshire*
3. Are you a British Subject?	3. *Yes*
4. What is your Age?	4. *18* Years. *...* Months.
5. What is your Trade or Calling?	5. *Labourer*
6. Have you resided out of your Father's house for three years continuously in the same place, or occupied a house or land of the yearly value of £10 for one year, and paid rates for the same, and, in either case, if so, state where	6. *14 yrs (2nd N. R.)*

You are hereby warned that if after enlistment it is found that you have given a wilfully false answer to any of the
following questions, you will be liable to a punishment of two years imprisonment with hard labour.

7. Are you, or have you been, an Apprentice? if so, where? to whom? and for what period?	7. *No*
8. Are you Married?	8. *No*
9. Have you ever been sentenced to Imprisonment by the Civil Power?	9. *No*
10. Do you now belong to Her Majesty's Army, the Militia, the Militia Reserve, the Royal Navy, the Volunteers, the Yeomanry, the Army Reserve, or the Naval Reserve Force? If so, to what Corps?	10. *No*
11. Have you ever served in Her Majesty's Army, the Marines, the Militia, the Militia Reserve, or the Royal Navy? If so, state which and cause of discharge	11. *No*
12. Have you ever been rejected as unfit from any of Her Majesty's Forces, with ignominy or as incorrigible and worthless, or on account of conviction of felony, or of a sentence of penal servitude, or have you been dismissed with disgrace from the Navy?	12.
13. Have you truly stated the whole, if any, of your previous Service?	13. *Yes*
14. Have you ever been rejected as unfit for Her Majesty's Service? If so, on what grounds?	14. *No*
15. Are you willing to be vaccinated or re-vaccinated?	15. *Yes*
16. For what Corps are you willing to be enlisted, or are you willing to be enlisted for General Service?	16. *Durham Light Infantry*
17. Did you receive a Notice, and do you understand its meaning, and who gave it to you?	17. *Yes.* (Name) *Sergt J. Booth* (Corps) *Grenr. Guards*

18. Are you willing to serve upon the following conditions
provided Her Majesty should so long require your service?

(a) For the term of Twelve years, for the first seven
years in Army Service, and for the remaining five years in the First
Class of the Army Reserve, or if, at the termination of such period
of Army Service, you are serving beyond the seas, then for the
first eight years in Army Service, and for the remaining four years
in the 1st Class of the Army Reserve.

(b) If, at the expiration of the above-mentioned term of
Army Service, whether of 7 or 8 years, a state of war exists, then, if
so directed by the competent Military Authority, to serve in Army
Service for a further period not exceeding 12 months.

(c) If, at the expiration of the above-mentioned term of
Army Service, you are so required by a proclamation from Her
Majesty in case of imminent national danger or great emergency, then
to serve in Army Service so as to complete your term of 12 years, and
for a further period not exceeding 12 months.

(d) If the above-mentioned term of 12 years expires
while you are on service with the Regular Forces beyond the seas, or
while a state of war exists with a Foreign Power, or while Soldiers in the
Reserve are required by proclamation to continue in or are recalled to
Army Service, then to serve for a further period not exceeding 12 months.

18.

I, *Thomas Chambers* do solemnly declare that the above answers made by me to
the above questions are true, and that I am willing to fulfil the engagements made.

Thomas Chambers Signature of Recruit. *Jas Booth Sergt* Signature of Wit...

OATH TO BE TAKEN BY RECRUIT ON ATTESTATION.

I, *Thomas Chambers* do make Oath, that I will be faithful and
bear true Allegiance to Her Majesty, Her Heirs, and Successors, and that I will, as in duty bound, honestly and faithfully
defend Her Majesty, Her Heirs, and Successors, in Person, Crown, and Dignity against all enemies, and will observe and
obey all orders of Her Majesty, Her Heirs, and Successors, and of the Generals and Officers set over me. So help me God.

Witness my hand. *Signature of Recruit* *Thomas Chambers*
Signature of Witness

CERTIFICATE OF MAGISTRATE OR ATTESTING OFFICER.

The Recruit above-named was cautioned by me that if he made any false answer to any of the above questions
he would be liable to be punished as provided in the Army Act.

The above questions were then read to the recruit in my presence.

I have taken care that he understands each question, and that his answer to each question has been duly entered as
replied to, and that recruit has made and signed the declaration and oath before me at *Derby*

on this *20* day of *October* 1894.

Signature of the Justice *H. Wood Colonel*

If any alteration is required on this page of the Attestation, a Justice of the Peace or Attesting Officer
under Section 80 (6), Army Act, 1881.

The Recruit should, if he require it, receive a copy of the Declaration on Army Form B. 93.

*Short Service – Attestation (page 1) of No. 5319 Thomas
Chambers.*

68

Chapter IV

1902

During the previous year Kitchener had been reducing the number of Boers in the field by about 1,000 per month. At this rate the war would have dragged on for many months. Whilst not an ideal short cut to the end of the War, Kitchener decided to increase the number of blockhouses and link them together by barbed wire, thereby creating a large grid-mesh of blockhouse lines, in order to speed up the end of the War. Within the perimeters of the fenced areas he would make a series of sweeps. These methods gradually undermined the fighting capacity of the Boers.

By May 1902 there would by 8,000 blockhouses in place covering in excess of 3,500 miles.

1 January
On Guard my first Block House.

5 January
What a dreary and anxious time this is, nothing else but funeral parties. What a terrible amount of deaths we are

having – only last week a L/Cpl in this tent was with me acting the part of a bearer for a Cpl. who had died and now himself is not expected to live. Truly one never knows the hour – how true are the words 'be ye always ready for we never know the day or the hour.' How I wish this fever season was over it makes one melancholy to see them sew the bodies in blankets and place them in the graves – the smell is enough to give one the fever.

13 January
Nothing of note. The same routine day after day. Outpost and Fatigues & Funerals rather too plentiful to be pleasant.

17 January
Paid out. Received £3. Quite a change to once more possess money.

19 January
Went out to station and had dinner. 3/6 [equiv. 17½p]. Like being at Home for once.

17 February
When we entrained at Middelberg at 5am. Reached Pretoria at 2pm where we took over 20 Boers and proceeded to Elandsfontein at 7.30pm. Reached Elandsfontein at 11.30pm where we took over 230 Boer prisoners of war mostly belonging to De Wets Commando.[1]

---

1 Christian de Wet (1854–1922), Boer General.

18 February
4.30am. Left Elandsfontein for Standerton arriving there at 3.30pm when we handed them over to an escort of the Mounted Infantry.

19 February
Stayed in Rest Camp all day. Tired out, no sleep for 3 nights – glad of the rest.

20 February
Remained in Rest Camp doing nothing.

21 February
Headquarters having arrived we went on Fatigue at 5.30am unloading baggage and finished at 7pm when a terrific thunderstorm came on and we just managed to have everything in Camp and under cover.

22 February
Breakfast for the Col. 9am parade at 10am. Went to Hospital for medical inspection and got garrison duty.

23 February
Fatigue in morning. Mounted Guard at night.

24 February
On Guard! Wrote two letters home. Magazine Ordinance Departure.

25 February
In camp doing nothing.

26 February
Mounted guard over prisoners of war. Took over 29.

27 February
On guard over prisoners. Sent 18 to Burgheth Camp.
Dismounted at 6pm.

28 February
Went Soldier's Home and wrote long letter to Blau
[Possibly a girlfriend].

Up to 13 March
When we left Standerton for Bankop. Marched to Lewes
Spruit for the night, a distance of 8 miles.

14 March
Marched off at 7.20 arrived at Ucheke at 4pm. Camped
for the night.

15 March
Marched off at 6.30 a distance of 15 miles.

16 March
Marched to Morgans Drift.

17 March
Marched off at 7.30 and arrived at Kaffir Spruit.

18 March
Marched off at 7.30 and arrived at Ermelo at 12.30 a
place of much importance owing to the many small
engagements fought in that neighbourhood. The town is in
ruins levelled to the ground by the British troops as it was
always a nest for the Boers.

19 March
Marched off at 7 a distance of 13 miles, halted and
camped for the night at Roodeval.

20 March
March off at 7 and arrived at Bankop 12 miles off – a
distance of 80 miles from Standerton.

21 March
Rested for the day.

22 March
Marched to No. 34 Blockhouse, midway between Ermelo
and Bankop, a distance of 8 miles where I took command
of 8 men and the Blockhouse. Our duties are composed of
digging trenches across the veldt all day and generally
passing the night in the trenches as the Boers are on either
side of us, so near that I fire into them every day. The
other night the Boers came to a Blockhouse about 500
yards and threw bombs into it blowing it up wounding
two men, the Boers taking their rifles, blankets etc. and
going, after politely asking them if there are any wounded

*and saying they were sorry. At the present time I am
making a network of wire on the top of my Blockhouse
which will throw the bomb off with a bounce and see if
that will keep us safe.*

23 March
*Rode into Ermelo and back, a distance of 30 miles for
supplies.*

24 March
Outpost at night, trench digging at daytime.

25 March
Digging trenches all day.

27 March
*Blau's birthday coming of age. I really thought I should
have been home for that but I was digging trenches across
the veldt all day. Nevertheless I am grateful I am still
alive and well and I am sure if it is God's will he will
take me back in his own good time. How I looked forward
to being at home for Blau's coming of age.*

22 April
*Eclipse of the moon I never saw the like. One minute up
and everything quite light when suddenly the moon went
out completely and where everything was daylight a few
minutes before the night was inky black. I never saw the
likes before.*

16 May
Marched to Bankop enroute to Athole Kop.

17 May
Athole.

18–23 May
Joined the construction column putting up Blockhouses towards Swaziland.

24 May
When I went into No 101 Blockhouse on the Swaziland border.

25 May
Today being Sunday I do not intend to do anything and as I am writing this I am hoping to shortly hear news of 'Peace'.

Talks of peace had been going on since mid-April when the Boers sent a delegation to Pretoria. However, there were disagreements between Sir Alfred Milner and Lord Kitchener on the terms to be negotiated which reflected the differing personal ambitions of the two men.

Kitchener wanted to see an end to the War as soon as possible, as did the British Government (almost at any price), whereas Milner did not accept the need to end the War. Milner was hoping for a clear-cut military victory which would give him a free hand to recast South Africa and deny forever the franchising of the natives. His original objective was to create a self-governing white community, supported by well-treated and justly governed black labour from Cape Town to the Zambezi.

Peace was eventually achieved on 31 May 1902 after a final meeting and acceptance by representatives of the Commandos, at Vereeniging. The terms were signed at Pretoria on the same day.

2 June
At last we have just got the official news of the declaration of peace, thank Heavens. I only hope we will soon go home now God being willing.

5 June
No rations – starving with hunger.

9 June
Received my first crime in the army – 7 years 8 months clear, for not complying with an order I have not received yet.

20 June
My birthday [age 27].

23 June
Moved to and took charge of 103 Blockhouse (Reserves went away).

26 June
Coronation Day. We have just got news festivities postponed owing to King being indisposed.

Demobilisation of the Battalion began on 1 July. The first troops to be dealt with were those who were time-expired men and reservists. They were sent down from Standerton to Eden Dale near Pietermaritzburg in detachments of 100. One of the last batches included Lance Corporal Chambers.

2 July
Marched off to Westhoe and bivouacked in a white frost.

3 July
Marched off to Bankop and bivouacked.

4 July
Marched to Roodeval and camped for the night.

5 July
Marched to Ermelo and camped.

6 July
Received a telegram from the Colonel to proceed immediately to Standerton.

7 July
Rode a distance of 30 miles towards Standerton.

8 July
Rode to Standerton a distance of 27 miles where I took
over the charge of Officers Mess and waited at dinner.

9 July–4 September
Mess Sergeant Durham Light Infantry till further orders
and remained doing the same till 5 September.

5 September
When I left for Pietermaritzburg for to proceed to
England, time expired arriving there at 4.30am.

7–12 September
Stayed at Pietermaritzburg.

12 September
Left Pietermaritzburg at 9.30pm and landed in Durban
6am. Embarked on board the Transport Englishman
staying in the harbour till Sunday 13th.

13 September
Left in tugs and crossed the harbour bar, the weather
being very rough and embarked on board the SS Sicilia
in a very rough sea, so rough that we could not get a
gangway across; had to wait till the waves drove the tug
close to the vessel then make a dart and climb up the
vessel sides by means of rope ladders, a very dangerous
game for men who had been used to the veldt for so long.
A slip meant death by being crushed in the sea between

the two boats. Left for Capetown at 6pm. Passed Port Elizabeth and arrived at Capetown 2pm 17.9.02 and proceeded to coal. Left Capetown 5pm for Las Palmas in splendid weather arriving there 2pm 3.10.02 and coaled, staying there for 8 hours principally watching the motley crew of hawkers in small boats round the vessel.

3 October
Left 10pm.

5 October
Passed the Magpie *cruising round the Spanish coast.*

7 October
Passed Finistere, rather rough in the Channel.

9 October
Arrived in Southampton at 12.30am and entrained for Newcastle on Tyne.

10 October
Arrived at Newcastle on Tyne at 2am where we had some bread and meat, received a blanket and lay down till 6am when we proceeded to Orderly Room – signed account.

9am. Received medal, £3, suit of clothes and took first train and reached home 8pm. The night I finished soldiering I hope for ever.

Just a small atom amongst the mighty crowd
that have returned from South Africa with
not a word of welcome to those who risked
their lives for the safety of England and her
countrymen. Give Honour where honour is due.

Although Chambers obviously felt that the returning soldiers were not appropriately welcomed back to England, the end of his military service was in fact the end of his service agreement and not the end of the War. This may well explain the lack of a suitable reception on his return, particularly as the troops, including those from the Durham Light Infantry, had returned in batches over quite an extended period of time, starting as far back as 31 July. Furthermore, the War itself had long ceased to occupy people's minds in the UK.

The Battalion, itself now much reduced, remained at Standerton until 26 October when it entrained for Durban and left for India on 29 October, arriving in Bombay thirteen days later.

Postscript

On the completion of his active military service in 1902 Thomas Chambers was *'transferred to the Reserve with an 8 years exemplary character finally to settle down to the life of Butler in a gentleman's house when I hope I have finished changing and hope soon to finish wandering to finally take unto myself a Wife.*

> *'To whom this book is to be dedicated when I hope I shall find that which so far in Life I have never received A faithful friend and helpmate.'*

Yours respectfully

C. T. Chambers

Epilogue

On leaving the army Thomas Chambers returned to civilian life as a butler in a gentleman's house thought to have been in Branksome Park, Bournemouth, on the South Coast. The circumstances of his move south are unknown.

However, although leaving the Army in October 1902, it did not take him long to find a wife as he was married in April 1903 to Martha Waltina Cross in St John's, the parish church of Tolpuddle, Dorset (the village of Tolpuddle martyrs fame) where she was born and brought up.

Although his birth certificate shows only one christian name, namely Thomas, he often referred to himself as Cecil Thomas and it was these two names which were recorded in the church marriage register.

Thomas and Martha Chambers had two sons, Cecil, who died in 1927 from peritonitis at the age of twenty-two years and Raymond Leslie, who died in 1995 at the age of eighty-five years.

Thomas Chambers was a butler for twelve years before once again becoming a soldier on the outbreak of the First World War, for the next four and half years.

He then spent twenty-four years as Steward at the Westover Club on Richmond Hill in Bournemouth, retiring in 1942. For the next three years he became a messenger with the Westminster Bank, retiring for the last time in 1945 at the age of seventy.

He died in 1953, having been married for fifty years.

*Thomas Chambers in his World War I uniform wearing his
South African campaign medals.*

84

Bibliography

Printed Sources

Black & White Budget   Vol. 1 & II and Vol. 3

Century Hutchinson   *The New World Encyclopedia*

Churchill, W.S.   *Young Winston's War*

Pakenham, T.   *The Boer War*

Pemberton, W.B.   *Battles of the Boer War*

Shaw, S.G.P.   *The Story of the Durham Light Infantry*

Vane, W.L.   *Durham Light Infantry*

Index

Almonds Nek, 45
Athole Kop, 75

Baden-Powell, Robert
  Stephenson Smyth, Col., 1, 42
Bankop, 72-3, 75, 77
Barton, Geoffrey, Maj. Gen., 15,
  23, 26
Bethal, 52
Biggarsberg, 37, 39-40
Blockhouses, 69, 73-6
Bloemfontein, 13
Bothas Pass, 45
Buller, Redvers, Gen. Sir, 2, 8, 13,
  15-16, 23, 30-1, 39, 53-4, 58
Burgheth Camp, 72

Charlestown, 45, 50
Chieveley, 8-9, 21
Chocolate Boxes, 32-4
Churchill, Winston, 7, 29-30
Clery, Cornelius Francis, Gen.
  Sir, 2, 22, 40, 54-7
Colenso, 8, 23, 65
Cooper C.D., Col., 32
Cronje, Pier, Gen., 13, 26-7, 29

Dannhauseer, 41
De Lisle, Capt., 3
Demobilisation, 77
De Wet, Christian, Gen., 70
Doornkloof, 19

Dublin Fusiliers, 23
Dundee, 1, 41
Durham Light Infantry, 2, 7, 18,
  20, 24, 60, 80

Eagles Nest, 24
Eden Kop, 56, 60-1
Elandsfontein, 66, 70
Elandslaagte, 1, 31, 34-7
Ermelo, 52, 73-4, 77
Estcourt, 7

FitzGerald, Lt. Col., 20, 52, 57
Fort Wiley, 23
7th Fusiliers, 4
Frere, 16

German Legion, 31
Green Hill, 23
Greylingstad, 53-5
Grobelaars Kloof, 24

Hamilton, Ian, Lt. Gen., 44
Hart, Arthur Fitzroy, Gen., 9
Heidelberg, 55, 61-2, 64, 66
Helpmakaar Pass, 41
Hildyard, Henry John Thomas,
  Gen., 21-2

Inkiuela, 42
Inniskilling Fusiliers, 24
Irish Brigade, 9-10, 24

Johannesburg, 44

Kaffir Spruit, 72
Kekewich, Robert, Lt. Col., 1
Kimberley, 1, 13
Kings Royal Rifle Corps, 7, 14, 37, 55
Kitchener, Lord, 12, 59, 62-3, 69, 75
Kroonstad, 39
Kruger, Stephanus, JP, 44

Ladysmith, 1, 8, 13, 16, 23, 27-30
Laings Nek, 39, 42, 44-7, 50, 52
Lambton, John, Gen., 20
Lambton, R.R., Lt., 20
Lewes Spruit, 72
Long Tom, 19, 21
Lyttleton, Maj. Gen., 2, 9, 15, 22, 32

Maconochie Kopjies, 15
Mafeking, 1, 39, 42-3
Magersfontein, 8
Mahon, Bryan, Col., 42
Majuba, 27, 42-4, 46-7
Middleberg, 66, 70
Milner, Alfred, Sir, 61, 75
Modder Spruit, 37
Monte Cristo, 22
Mooi River, 6, 61
Morgans Drift, 72
Mount Alice, 14, 21
Mount Prospect, 42
Mounted Infantry, 3-4

Newcastle (Natal), 42
Nicholson's Nek, 1
Norcott, Col., 22

O'Neill's Farm, 52
Orange Free State, 8, 43

Paardeberg, 13, 29
Paarde Kop, 50
Parke, Capt., 38
Pietermaritzburg, 77-8
Pieters Hill, 23-6
Platrand, 51
Plummer, Herbert, Lt. Col., 42
Potgieters Drift, 14, 16-17
Pretoria, 39, 44-5, 53-4, 66, 70
Pugwagne, 42-4

Railway Hill, 24-6
Rasbotham, Lt., 63
1st Rifle Brigade, 6, 26, 55
Roberts, Lord, 10, 12, 26, 29, 39, 44-5, 53-4, 57-8
Roberts F.H.S., Lt. Hon., 9
Roodeval, 73, 77
Royal Welsh Fusiliers, 22

St Helena, 27, 63
Scots Fusiliers, 4
2nd Scottish Rifles, 7, 55
Shafto, C.D., Lt., 20
South African Light Horse, 37
Spearmans Hill, 14
Spion Kop, 13-15
Springfield, 14
Standerton, 39, 50-2, 54-7, 61, 66, 71, 77-8
Stormberg, 8

Transvaal, 27, 57
Tugela, 8, 14-15

Ucheke, 72

Vaal Krantz, 6, 17-18, 20, 52
Vaal Laaghe, 53
Vaal River, 44
Vereeniging, 76
Vlakfontein, 53-6
Volkrust, 45-50

Warren, Charles, Sir, 13, 15, 26

Waschbank River, 40
Waterval, 56
Westhoe, 77
White, George, Lt. Gen., 1, 28, 30
Willow Grange, 7
Woodland, Col., 18, 57

Zand Spruit, 50